Mind Over Code

Avoid Burnout and Boost Your Brain as a Developer

Emma Royce Smartley

Copyright © 2024 Emma Royce Smartley

All rights reserved.

DEDICATION

This book is dedicated to those developers who push limits, shape the future, and provide solutions to tomorrow's challenges. I hope it motivates you to put your health first, stoke your enthusiasm, and maintain mental clarity while you navigate the trials that lie ahead.

I also want to express my gratitude to my mentors, family, and friends for their constant belief in me and support. Every action I've taken has been based on your encouragement.

CONTENTS

ACKNOWLEDGMENTS 1

CHAPTER 1 1

How Long Coding Sessions Affect Brain Function 1

    1.1 The Overworking Culture 1

    1.2 Lack of Sleep and Cognitive Decline 3

    1.3 Emotional Fatigue and Burnout 5

CHAPTER 2 9

The Effects of Not Being Active 9

    2.1 The Lifestyle of the Sedentary Developer 9

    2.2 The Benefits of Exercise for the Brain 10

    2.3 Inactivity's Dangers to the Health of the Brain and Body 13

CHAPTER 3 17

Ignoring Mental Exercise When Not at Work 17

    3.1 The Stagnation Trap 17

    3.2 The Value of Lifelong Education 18

    3.3 Cognitive Decline's Perils 21

CHAPTER 4 24

The Developer's Isolation 24

    4.1 Isolation from Others in the Tech Sector 24

    4.2 Social Interaction's Cognitive Benefits 26

    4.3 The Effects of Loneliness on the Mind 28

CHAPTER 5 32

Developers' Sleep and Cognitive Function 32

5.1 Sleep's Function in Brain Health.. 32

5.2 Developers Who Constantly Lack Sleep....................................... 35

5.3 Sleeping Habits and Recuperation.. 37

CHAPTER 6..42

Stress Management and Brain Activity.....................................42

6.1 The Developmental Environment Under High Stress................... 42

6.2 The Reaction of the Brain to Prolonged Stress............................ 44

6.3 Developer Stress-Reduction Strategies...................................... 47

CHAPTER 7..53

Diet and Mental Well-Being... 53

7.1 Developers' Unhealthy Eating Patterns.......................................53

7.2 Foods That Improve the Brain.. 56

7.3 Hydration's Function.. 59

CHAPTER 8..63

Brain Fatigue and Digital Overload.. 63

8.1 Continuous Screen Time.. 63

8.2 The Effects of Information Overload... 65

8.3 Methods for Reducing Digital Fatigue... 68

CHAPTER 9..73

Work-Life Balance's Significance... 73

9.1 The Stress of Personal Sacrifice and Deadlines...........................73

9.2 Leisure's Contribution to Cognitive Health.................................. 76

9.3 Setting Work and Life Boundaries.. 78

CHAPTER 10..82

Developing Healthful Routines for Long-Term Mental Well-Being..... 82

10.1 Establishing a Healthful Habit 82

10.2 Including Mental and Social Input 85

10.3 The Advantages of a Balanced Lifestyle Over Time 88

ABOUT THE AUTHOR **91**

ACKNOWLEDGMENTS

First and foremost, I would like to sincerely thank everyone who helped me along the way as I wrote this book. This trip was made possible by your support and faith in my goal.

I want to express my gratitude to my family for their love, support, and tolerance as I spent many hours writing. My strength has always come from your support.

To my friends and IT sector colleagues: thank you for your tremendous thoughts, experiences, and feedback that have inspired the content of this book. I appreciate you sharing your knowledge and giving me a new perspective on the development community.

To the mentors and thought leaders whose studies and expertise have influenced these pages: I am incredibly appreciative of your contributions to the profession, and your work keeps pushing the envelope of what is feasible.

Lastly, I would want to thank all of the readers for reading this book. I hope it gives you the direction and resources you need to go through your own path with a mind that is thriving and healthy.

CHAPTER 1

How Long Coding Sessions Affect Brain Function

1.1 The Overworking Culture

There is a pervasive culture of overworking in the computer sector, especially among software developers. It is common to see putting in long hours, working on the weekends, and staying up late to achieve deadlines as a sign of honor. It is common to romanticize this "hustle culture," in which developers brag about their capacity to produce code in long coding sessions, sometimes without much sleep.

This exaltation of overwork has been influenced by a number of factors:

- **Competitive pressure:** Developers frequently feel they must outperform their peers in high-stakes settings, like startups or big tech companies, in order to stay relevant or land promotions.

- **Technological advancements:** Developers are continuously connected thanks to remote work and always-on devices, which further blurs the lines between work and rest.

- **Personal pride:** Many developers are proud of their ability to solve problems, and they may experience a sense of personal achievement when they stay up late trying to "fix that one bug."

- **External expectations:** Developers are often pushed to extend their workdays in order to fulfill irrational deadlines by clients, management, and stakeholders who demand speedier turnarounds.

The long-term consequences on brain health can be disastrous, even though this culture may occasionally result in brief increases in productivity. Long-term overwork not only wears out the body but also severely strains cognitive functions, which eventually results in decreased productivity. This part lays the groundwork for comprehending the serious emotional and neurological effects of long-term overwork in the computer industry.

1.2 Lack of Sleep and Cognitive Decline

Despite the fact that sleep is crucial for brain function, developers usually forego it in favor of longer workdays. Numerous studies have demonstrated that sleep deprivation causes serious cognitive impairments, especially when it comes to the brain's capacity to operate at its best.

1. **Memory Consolidation:** Sleep is important for memory consolidation. The brain organizes and integrates the knowledge acquired during the day while you are in deep sleep. Developers who don't get enough sleep have a far harder time remembering new information, such as complicated algorithms, debugging techniques, or new programming languages. They can therefore find themselves making the same mistakes over and over again or having to relearn knowledge that didn't stick because they didn't get enough sleep.
2. **Attention Span:** Lack of sleep also impairs attention

and focus. Long stretches of focused attention are frequently needed for coding, but when people don't get enough sleep, their attention spans shorten and they make mistakes and get distracted more easily. Because the brain finds it difficult to sustain the cognitive endurance required to stay on task, tasks that should take minutes may take hours.

3. **Capabilities for Making Decisions:** Making decisions all the time is necessary when writing clear, effective code. Every coding session involves hundreds of micro-decisions, from selecting the appropriate data structures to determining implementation tactics. However, brains that are sleep deprived have trouble making decisions. Developers can end up making snap decisions, overlooking important details, or losing sight of the wider picture problems that could have been prevented with enough sleep.

Chronic sleep deprivation has been associated with cognitive loss over time. Slower processing rates, trouble multitasking, and diminished problem-solving skills are some of the ways this can show up. These skills are crucial for software development. These cognitive impairments might compound over time, resulting in lower output and lower-quality work.

1.3 Emotional Fatigue and Burnout

Long coding sessions have an emotional cost that goes well beyond cognitive deterioration and physical fatigue. Overworking is frequently accompanied by burnout, a condition of ongoing emotional and mental tiredness. The emotional and psychological effects of overtaxing the brain are examined in this section.

- **Stress and Anxiety:** Developers who are under continual pressure to fulfill deadlines may feel more stressed. The constant loop of problem fixes, code debugging, and time pressure can cause chronic stress, which has a detrimental effect on the brain. Constant stress causes the brain to release the hormone cortisol, which can harm the prefrontal cortex of the brain and impair executive and decision-making abilities when it is present in high concentrations. This traps developers in a vicious cycle of decreasing returns by further impairing cognitive function and creativity.

- **Mood Regulation:** Long coding hours and lack of sleep also have an impact on mood regulation. When the brain is overloaded, emotional resilience deteriorates. Irritability or annoyance can result from little setbacks, such a program not compiling successfully or a challenging problem taking longer than anticipated. Developers may become more reactive, impatient, or even emotionally distant from their work as a result of this emotional exhaustion over time.

- **Loss of Creativity:** Coding necessitates creativity, especially when it comes to invention or problem-solving. Burnout, however, exhausts the brain capacity required for original thought. Burnout can lead to creative slumps in developers, making it difficult for them to think creatively or come up with novel ideas. This lack of motivation can be especially discouraging in a field where innovative problem-solving is essential.

- **Apathy and Emotional Detachment:** As burnout worsens, developers may start to feel emotionally detached from their work; this is known as depersonalization. They could be skeptical, uninspired, or disconnected from their projects. Although this emotional distance serves as a coping strategy for the extreme strain, it eventually results in poorer performance and less job satisfaction.

Burnout and emotional exhaustion have far-reaching long-term effects. In addition to losing their enthusiasm and inventiveness for their profession, developers can suffer from memory loss, poorer brain function, and even a higher risk of mental health conditions like anxiety and depression. Maintaining emotional and cognitive health in a field that requires a high degree of intellectual engagement requires identifying and resolving the early indicators of burnout.

The impact of long coding sessions on brain health cannot be exaggerated, even though they may seem like an essential component of tech culture. Developers are at a high risk of long-term mental and physical health problems due to the culture of overworking, cognitive deterioration from sleep deprivation, and the emotional toll of burnout. Developers and organizations must question the status paradigm and cultivate a work culture that prioritizes relaxation, recuperation, and sustainable working methods if they want to genuinely maximize productivity and maintain brain health.

CHAPTER 2

The Effects of Not Being Active

2.1 The Lifestyle of the Sedentary Developer

Long desk hours are common in the fast-paced field of software development. Developers frequently spend a lot of time sitting down writing code or addressing complicated problems. Although this sedentary lifestyle has been ingrained in the industry, there are serious physical and mental health concerns associated with it.

Whether at their workstation, in meetings, or on their commute, the typical developer may spend 8 to 12 hours a day sitting down. The "sedentary developer lifestyle," a pattern of behavior marked by little physical activity, is a result of such extended periods of inactivity. Among the contributing elements are:

1. **Work demands:** Hours spent in front of a screen with little respite are frequently the consequence of

strict deadlines, difficult projects, and the ongoing need to troubleshoot and debug code.
2. **Focus and flow:** When developers are "in the zone," they may lose track of time and choose working continuously over getting up or taking brief breaks to move around.
3. **Remote work:** As remote work has become more popular, many developers are working from home instead of walking or commuting to the office, which further reduces daily physical activity.

Long periods of sitting cause a number of problems that developers might not notice right away. Joint pain, particularly in the neck and back, poor posture, and muscular stiffness are all exacerbated by prolonged immobility. Hours of sitting can also slow down metabolism, increasing the risk of metabolic illnesses and causing weight gain. In addition to these health hazards, sedentary lifestyles have significant effects on brain function that are frequently disregarded.

2.2 The Benefits of Exercise for the Brain

It is commonly known that physical activity and brain health are related. Research indicates that frequent physical activity is essential for sustaining and improving cognitive functions, despite developers' belief that mental work solely takes cognitive effort. This section examines how exercise can directly help development and enhance brain function.

It has been demonstrated that physical activity, especially aerobic workouts like walking, jogging, or cycling, increases the production of brain-derived neurotrophic factor (BDNF), which in turn improves memory. In order to boost memory and learning capacities, BDNF is essential for encouraging the growth and survival of neurons. Whether it's learning a new programming language, remembering complex system designs, or managing several project tasks, developers who have greater memory are able to retain more knowledge.

- **Enhanced Focus and Attention:** Exercise improves focus and attention span by increasing blood flow to the brain. Regular exercise helps developers focus better, which makes it easier for them to work quickly and pay attention to details throughout lengthy coding sessions. According to studies, even brief physical activity bursts, such as a brisk walk, can enhance cognitive control, enabling people to switch activities more skillfully and stay distracted-free.

- **Improved Problem-Solving Ability:** Physical exercise also improves creativity and problem-solving abilities. Exercise causes dopamine and endorphins to be released, which improve mood and foster mental clarity. For engineers who must think critically and tackle difficult problems on a regular basis, this mental clarity is very crucial. Developers may discover that they are better able to tackle challenging code problems with new ideas and creative solutions after engaging in physical exercise.

Additionally, exercise encourages neurogenesis, or the growth of new neurons in the brain, which can improve brain plasticity in general. For developers in particular, this is advantageous because rapid learning and adaptation are essential in the ever changing world of technology.

2.3 Inactivity's Dangers to the Health of the Brain and Body

Beyond weight gain and muscular stiffness, physical inactivity has serious negative effects on body and mental health. Sedentary lifestyles put developers at higher risk for a number of chronic illnesses that can affect their general health and cognitive abilities.

- **Metabolic disorders and obesity:** Long-term inactivity slows down metabolism, which increases the risk of obesity and makes weight gain easier. Inflammation has been connected to excess body fat, especially visceral fat, and this can have a detrimental effect on brain function. Insulin resistance, a prelude to type 2 diabetes, is also linked to obesity. It has been demonstrated that insulin resistance affects brain functioning, especially memory and cognitive flexibility, which are critical abilities for software developers.

- **Cardiovascular Disease:** Heart disease, stroke, and hypertension are among the cardiovascular disorders for which inactivity is a significant risk factor. Over time, cognitive loss results from poor circulation and high blood pressure, which limit the quantity of oxygen and nutrients that reach the brain. Because proper brain function depends on the effective transport of oxygen and nutrients via blood flow, developers must have a healthy circulatory system.

- **Mental Sluggishness:** People who are not active frequently complain of mental sluggishness, brain fog, and diminished cognitive acuity. This is partially because neurotransmitters like dopamine and serotonin, which are essential for controlling mood, energy levels, and mental clarity, are produced less when people are physically inactive. Physically inactive developers may therefore experience decreased productivity, slowed reaction times, and trouble focusing on challenging tasks.

- **Mood Disorders:** A higher incidence of mood disorders like anxiety and sadness is also associated with inactivity. By encouraging the release of endorphins and lowering stress hormones like cortisol, exercise has been shown to reduce the symptoms of depression. Frequent exercise lowers the risk of mental health problems, enhances sleep quality, and helps control mood. Maintaining mental health is essential for developers because anxiety and sadness can significantly hinder motivation, creativity, and problem-solving skills.

Chronic inactivity has been linked over time to neurodegenerative illnesses such as Parkinson's and Alzheimer's. These disorders considerably lower quality of life in addition to impairing brain function. Developers may protect their physical and mental well-being and maintain their professional acuity for years to come by integrating regular exercise into their daily routines.

Developers' sedentary lifestyles present significant hazards to their bodily and emotional well-being. Chronic diseases that impair creativity and productivity, emotional disorders, and cognitive decline can result from prolonged sitting and inactivity. However, adding regular exercise to daily routines can greatly improve focus, memory, problem-solving abilities, and brain function in general. As a vital tool for long-term success and wellbeing in the IT sector, developers who depend on their cognitive abilities to perform well should place a high priority on physical activity.

CHAPTER 3

IGNORING MENTAL EXERCISE WHEN NOT AT WORK

3.1 The Stagnation Trap

To keep up with the demands of their profession, developers in the rapidly changing industry of software development are always learning new tools, frameworks, and languages. But frequently, this learning is restricted to what is immediately required for work-related tasks. This strategy may eventually result in intellectual stagnation. Developers run the danger of losing out on the wider mental stimulation that fosters holistic brain development and growth when they limit their learning to only work-related tasks.

Because stagnation frequently poses as productivity, it is an especially pernicious trap. Mastering the newest coding language or resolving a challenging technical issue at work may make a developer feel accomplished, but if all intellectual endeavors are linked to urgent professional requirements, there won't be much opportunity for creative or cognitive growth outside that limited scope. This leads to a cycle in which the same kinds of tasks repeatedly test the developer's brain, eventually causing mental rigidity.

This stagnation carries risks on both a personal and professional level. When developers must move to a new domain outside of their comfort zone or deal with unfamiliar difficulties, they may find that their adaptability decreases. Additionally, because the brain requires variety and novelty in thought, a lack of mental stimulation outside of work can result in boredom, disengagement, and even burnout. Without pushing themselves outside of work, developers unintentionally restrict their ability to be creative, innovative, and problem-solving.

3.2 The Value of Lifelong Education

Sustaining cognitive flexibility and wellness requires lifelong learning. Constant mental stimulation is essential for brain fitness, just as physical exercise is for maintaining physical fitness. The brain can stay flexible, sharp, and able to handle a variety of problems by participating in activities that activate different parts of the brain.

Beyond their regular profession, developers can pursue lifelong learning in a variety of ways:

1. The brain is exposed to fresh concepts, diverse viewpoints, and critical thinking exercises when one reads books on subjects other than software development, such as philosophy, history, or science. While fiction helps develop empathy and emotional intelligence, non-fiction can help us comprehend the world better.
2. **Puzzles & Brain Games:** Sudoku, crosswords, chess, and even strategy-based video games push the brain to think in new ways, which improves logical reasoning, memory, and pattern recognition.
3. **Learning New Skills:** Learning a new skill or hobby, like painting, speaking a foreign language, or playing an instrument, stimulates other portions of the brain that might not be used for regular coding jobs. By encouraging neuroplasticity the brain's capacity to create and rearrange synaptic connections this variety maintains the health of the

brain.

Lifelong learning has advantages that go beyond mental well-being. Diverse mental exercises improve problem-solving skills, encourage creativity, and strengthen emotional resilience. Developers who keep learning new topics outside of their line of work are typically more creative, flexible, and better able to deal with difficult or unforeseen problems. A developer who routinely pursues artistic endeavors, for instance, might approach coding difficulties more creatively and unconventionally than someone who only concentrates on technical understanding.

Additionally, a sense of accomplishment and personal contentment are enhanced by lifelong learning. Developers can avoid boredom or complacency, sustain curiosity, and stay passionate about their profession and personal lives by always learning new things. The secret to long-term pleasure and job satisfaction is this feeling of development and achievement.

3.3 Cognitive Decline's Perils

There can be major repercussions if you don't participate in a variety of mental activities outside of work, especially when it comes to cognitive decline. The gradual loss of mental skills like memory, logic, and problem-solving is known as cognitive decline, and it can occur when the brain is not sufficiently challenged or stimulated.

Decreased creativity is one of the main dangers of cognitive decline. Developers may experience a decline in their ability to think creatively if they do not broaden their mental horizons outside of work. Exposure to novel concepts and other ways of thinking fosters creativity. It becomes more difficult to think creatively or approach problems from new angles when the brain is continuously involved in the same kinds of problem-solving exercises.

Neglecting mental stimulation might impair not only creativity but also problem-solving abilities. Although developers may become quite specialized in their technical work, they may lose the capacity for critical thought or problem-solving when faced with challenges beyond their area of expertise. It becomes more difficult to adjust to novel circumstances, pick up new technologies fast, or come up with creative solutions when cognitive flexibility is lost. Developers may find it difficult to progress in their careers or take on more challenging responsibilities as a result of the long-term professional plateau.

Like any other organ, the brain needs regular exercise to stay healthy. The brain's capacity to create new connections is weakened in the absence of varied mental demands, increasing its vulnerability to age-related decline. There are several ways that cognitive impairment might appear, including:

1. **Memory Issues:** Inability to quickly pick up new skills, retain tasks, or recall information.
2. **Decreased Focus:** The inability to focus or pay attention for extended periods of time.
3. **Diminished Decision-Making:** Slower information processing results in less confident problem-solving and worse decision-making.

Furthermore, stress and dissatisfaction can rise as a result of cognitive impairment and mental stagnation. Increased emotional exhaustion might further impede cognitive abilities like memory and focus in those who feel stalled or uninspired. This cycle of deterioration and stagnation might eventually have a detrimental effect on one's personal and professional well-being.

Developers run serious dangers when they overlook mental stimulation outside of work. The brain thrives on variety, novelty, and ongoing learning, even if the demands of software development frequently call for strong concentration on particular talents. Developers who exclusively concentrate on work-related tasks run the risk of becoming stagnant and eventually losing their creativity, problem-solving skills, and cognitive wellness. Developers must make lifelong learning and mental stimulation a priority in their personal lives, partaking in activities that test various parts of their brains, in order to mitigate these hazards. They can continue to be creative, retain their cognitive flexibility, and experience lifelong personal and professional fulfillment by doing this.

CHAPTER 4

The Developer's Isolation

4.1 Isolation from Others in the Tech Sector

The nature of software development frequently necessitates extended periods of intense, concentrated work, which results in extended periods of isolation. Code writing, debugging, and complicated problem-solving are common tasks for developers that need focus and little outside distraction. Despite being productive, this setting may unintentionally result in social isolation. Although engineers may engage online through team chats or collaborative tools, this isolation is not usually immediately apparent because significant in-person human interaction is rarely replaced by digital interaction.

Particularly in the computer sector, there is a culture that occasionally encourages or even romanticizes working alone. The image of the lone programmer, cooped up in a room for days on end, working diligently to solve a complex problem, has come to represent intellect and commitment. This picture conceals the negative impacts of extended seclusion on mental and emotional health, even if it may appear empowering or glamorous.

Developers who operate under these circumstances may eventually start to feel cut off from their friends, family, and coworkers. The advent of remote labor, which has become more prevalent in the tech sector, exacerbates this divide. Developers risk progressively losing touch with their social network, both personally and professionally, if they are deprived of the casual social interactions that take place in a physical office setting, such as lunch breaks, casual discussions, or simply commuting.

Social isolation poses a threat not just to one's mental well-being but also to one's capacity for innovation and teamwork. Even while it requires concentrated work, software development also benefits greatly from collaboration and idea exchange. Developers lose out on important brainstorming sessions, group problem-solving, and the sharing of different viewpoints that might result in more creative solutions when they don't regularly engage with others.

4.2 Social Interaction's Cognitive Benefits

Maintaining cognitive health requires human interaction, which is especially important for developers who work alone for extended periods of time. Participating in social activities and meaningful interactions activates different parts of the brain, which fosters problem-solving abilities, emotional intelligence, and cognitive flexibility. Social engagement increases the brain's neuroplasticity by fostering the formation of new connections, whether through light conversation or in-depth discussions.

There are various important categories into which the cognitive advantages of social engagement can be divided:

1. **Enhanced Memory and Learning:** Participating in conversations with others exposes developers to fresh viewpoints, ideas, and experiences that can strengthen their memory and increase their comprehension of many subjects. Discussions that

entail elucidating ideas, instructing others, or arguing points of view force the brain to retain knowledge and exercise critical thought, which improves learning ability.

2. **Enhanced Problem-Solving:** Group conversations frequently yield ideas that would not be obtained separately. Developers can gain from the group's collective intelligence by discussing issues with friends or coworkers, which may result in more creative and efficient solutions. Social connection helps developers see problems from multiple perspectives and fosters creative thinking.

3. **Emotional Regulation:** Emotional well-being, which has a direct effect on cognitive function, also depends on human contact. By lowering stress, promoting a sense of belonging, and offering emotional support, meaningful social connections aid in the regulation of emotions. Developers are more robust to obstacles when they have a sense of community, which improves their ability to concentrate and make decisions.

Developers can also relax and rejuvenate their minds by

engaging in social activities outside of work, such going to social gatherings, joining clubs, or taking part in group hobbies. By providing a counterweight to the solitary nature of coding, these activities aid in avoiding cognitive weariness and burnout.

To put it briefly, frequent social interaction serves as a brain workout. Social interaction improves the brain's capacity to assimilate information, adjust to novel circumstances, and sustain emotional balance, just like physical training does for muscles.

4.3 The Effects of Loneliness on the Mind

Long-term isolation frequently results in loneliness, which offers serious threats to one's mental and cognitive well-being, even though occasional solitude can help with concentration and productivity. More than just a sense of isolation, loneliness is a psychological condition in which a person feels cut off from other people and can result in a variety of detrimental emotional and psychological effects.

Because developers work alone, the psychological effects

of loneliness can be especially noticeable for them. Feelings of loneliness can be exacerbated by the long hours spent coding, frequently in quiet or with little to no human connection. If this loneliness is not addressed, it may develop into more serious mental health conditions including anxiety and depression.

- **Depression:** Depression is often associated with social isolation and loneliness. Developers who spend too much time alone may become disengaged from their social surroundings and experience depressive, hopeless, or useless feelings. Because depression can affect cognitive abilities like memory, focus, and judgment, developers may find it more difficult to work at their best.

- **Anxiety:** Lack of social interaction can also make developers more anxious since they may become overly focused on their work and worry about performance, deadlines, or the caliber of their output. Anxiety can worsen in the absence of social support to discuss these worries, leading to physical and mental symptoms such as weariness, difficulty focusing, and restlessness.

Loneliness has a psychological impact on cognitive function in addition to emotional well-being. According to studies, long-term loneliness might cause cognitive deterioration since social connections provide the brain with stimulus. Lack of consistent social interaction lowers the brain's neuroplasticity, which can hinder critical thinking, creativity, and learning new things.

Furthermore, loneliness raises stress levels, which in turn may cause the body's stress response hormone cortisol to be released. Long-term exposure to elevated cortisol levels can harm brain tissue, especially in regions like the hippocampus that are involved in memory and learning. This may eventually result in mental sluggishness and a reduction in cognitive function in general.

Developers must promote social connection, even in minor ways, to reduce the psychological and cognitive hazards associated with loneliness. This might entail:
1. Maintaining a sense of community can be achieved by arranging frequent check-ins with friends, family,

or coworkers.
2. **Taking part in team-building exercises** in order to develop more solid professional connections.
3. To keep in touch with people, consider joining online communities or interest groups centered around interests or hobbies.

Even though coding necessitates a great deal of concentrated, lonely work, it's important to recognize the loneliness that frequently accompanies this line of work. Social isolation puts developers at risk for cognitive and mental deterioration. Maintaining brain health, improving creativity, and avoiding emotions of loneliness and exhaustion all depend on social connection. Developers can safeguard their mental health, improve their cognitive function, and live more balanced, satisfying lives by trying to participate in important social activities.

CHAPTER 5

Developers' Sleep and Cognitive Function

One of the most essential biological processes for preserving general health, particularly brain function, is sleep. Because they are frequently enmeshed in the cycle of extended coding sessions and strict deadlines, developers may fail to see how important sleep is to maintaining their cognitive capacities. This chapter will examine the relationship between sleep and brain health, the effects of long-term sleep deprivation on development, and doable methods for enhancing sleep patterns to promote longevity and cognitive recovery.

5.1 Sleep's Function in Brain Health

The brain is in a highly active state throughout sleep, which is essential for sustaining a variety of cognitive processes. Sleep is not only a time for the body to relax. The brain goes through a number of changes while we sleep that improve our ability to function effectively while we are up. Consolidation of memories, emotional control, creativity, and general cognitive renewal are some of these processes.

Sleep plays a crucial part in memory consolidation, which is one of its most important roles. Deep sleep allows the brain to assimilate and integrate new information that has been learned throughout the day, especially during the REM (rapid eye movement) stage. This practice helps developers, who are often learning new programming languages, frameworks, or debugging techniques, improve their coding abilities and remember key information. Lack of sleep causes this consolidation to be insufficient, which results in memory lapses and a diminished ability to learn.

- **Emotional Balance:** Sleep is important for controlling emotions as well. High-pressure developers may feel stressed, frustrated, or anxious, all of which can affect their ability to make creative and sound decisions. Better emotional resilience and balance are promoted by a full night of restorative sleep, which resets the brain's emotional circuitry.

For developers, who frequently work under pressure to fulfill project deadlines or resolve challenging technical problems, this is especially crucial. Lack of sleep increases the risk of burnout by making it more difficult to manage stress.

- **Creativity and Solving Problems:** Creativity and sleep are closely related, and developers who are expected to write creative code or come up with original solutions to technical problems need to get enough sleep. During sleep, the brain restructures and reorganizes information, enabling fresh connections and insights that are essential for innovative problem-solving. Well-rested developers are better able to think creatively, debug more successfully, and generate code that is cleaner and more effective.

All things considered, sleep acts as a cognitive reset, readying the brain to perform at its best the following day. Developers are compromising their own productivity and mental clarity when they forgo sleep in favor of longer workdays.

5.2 Developers Who Constantly Lack Sleep

Developers frequently compromise their sleep because of the pressures of the IT business, considering it a luxury rather than a need. Consistently receiving less than seven hours of sleep per night is known as chronic sleep deprivation, and it can have detrimental effects on long-term brain health, productivity, and cognitive performance.

- **Impaired Cognitive Function:** Research indicates that sleep deprivation dramatically impairs cognitive function, especially in domains like decision-making, attentiveness, and reaction time. Developers who get little sleep frequently have trouble focusing, which causes them to code more slowly and make more mistakes. The cumulative consequences of sleep deprivation can cause a discernible deterioration in one's capacity for original thought and problem-solving over time.

- **A reduction in neuroplasticity:** Sleep is crucial for

neuroplasticity, the brain's capacity to change and create new connections. Less neuroplasticity may make it more difficult for developers to meet corporate standards, as their work necessitates constant learning and technological adaptability. Lack of sleep impairs the brain's ability to create and fortify new synaptic connections, which makes it more difficult to remember knowledge and pick up new abilities.

- **Risks to Long-Term Brain Health:** Chronic sleep deprivation can cause long-term problems with brain health in addition to short-term cognitive performance. Lack of sleep has been connected to a higher risk of neurodegenerative illnesses like dementia and Alzheimer's. Regular sleep deprivation may put children at risk for these disorders, which can negatively affect their quality of life as they age.

- **Emotional and Physical tiredness:** Chronic sleep deprivation causes mood swings, impatience, and emotional tiredness in addition to cognitive impairment. Developers who put in a lot of overtime under these circumstances are more likely to experience stress and burnout, which has an impact on their general well-being, professional relationships, and mental health.

These problems can be made worse by the IT industry's "hustle" culture, which normalizes working excessive hours to meet deadlines. The costs of forgoing sleep in favor of productivity, however, are high because developers can't sustain optimal performance over time.

5.3 Sleeping Habits and Recuperation

Given how important sleep is for mental and emotional well-being, developers should make sleep a priority in their self-care regimen. The good news is that many of the detrimental consequences of sleep deprivation can be reversed by enhancing sleep habits and concentrating on recuperation. The following useful advice will help you maintain better sleep hygiene and make sure your brain gets the rest it requires:

- **Create a Regular Sleep Schedule:** Keeping a

regular sleep-wake cycle is one of the best strategies to enhance the quality of your sleep. The body's internal clock is regulated when bedtime and wake-up times are consistent, which facilitates falling asleep and waking up feeling rejuvenated. Developers should make an effort to maintain their schedule even on the weekends to prevent interfering with their sleep cycle.

- **Create a Restful Sleep Environment:** The environment in which sleep occurs has a significant impact on its quality. By reducing noise, obstructing light, and maintaining a reasonable temperature, developers can make sure their bedrooms are restful. It's also critical to limit the amount of time spent using gadgets (such phones, laptops, or tablets) before bed because the blue light they emit can disrupt the production of melatonin, the hormone that controls sleep.

- **Restrict the use of stimulants and work at night:** Nicotine, caffeine, and other stimulants can disrupt sleep, particularly if they are used late in the day.

Developers who use energy drinks or coffee to get through coding sessions should watch how much they consume, especially in the hours before bed. Developers should also make an effort to avoid working through the night. The cycle of sleep deprivation may be prolonged by the mental excitement that comes from coding or solving problems, which can make it more difficult to relax and go to sleep.

- Incorporate techniques for relaxation. The secret to improved sleep is stress management. Developers may find it helpful to include relaxation methods in their bedtime regimen, such as progressive muscle relaxation, deep breathing, or meditation. By lowering anxiety and encouraging relaxation, these techniques assist in calming the mind and getting the body ready for sound sleep.

- **Regular Exercise:** By lowering stress and encouraging deeper sleep stages, exercise can enhance the quality of your sleep. However, because it can have a stimulating effect, individuals should avoid doing strenuous exercise right before bed. Rather, adding little exercise earlier in the day, like yoga, cycling, or walking, can improve the quality of your sleep and help you manage your sleep-wake cycle.

- **Nap Strategically:** Although naps can provide you a short energy boost, you should utilize them wisely to prevent them from interfering with your sleep at night. For those who are feeling exhausted during the day, a quick 20–30 minute nap in the early afternoon may be beneficial. Longer or later-in-the-day naps, however, may make it more difficult to fall asleep at night.

The Value of Recuperation

Maintaining long-term cognitive performance requires incorporating frequent mental and physical recuperation periods. Developers who place a high value on relaxation and recuperation, including getting enough sleep, are more likely to retain their emotional fortitude, creativity, and problem-solving abilities. Sleep enables the brain to recuperate from stress, process and integrate information, and get ready for the demands of the following day.

Sleep is an essential component of cognitive performance and brain health, especially for developers. Long-term sleep deprivation impairs mental health, creativity, and productivity. Developers may safeguard their brain health, increase their performance, and have more balanced, satisfying careers by realizing the value of sleep and implementing techniques to optimize sleep habits.

CHAPTER 6

STRESS MANAGEMENT AND BRAIN ACTIVITY

Stress is practically a given in the fast-paced field of software development. This field of work can be extremely stressful due to strict deadlines, intricate problem-solving, and the constantly evolving technological landscape. While a certain amount of stress might spur productivity, prolonged, unchecked stress can seriously impair cognitive function and brain health. This chapter explores how stress affects development, how the brain reacts to extended stress, and practical methods for lowering stress to preserve brain health.

6.1 The Developmental Environment Under High Stress

High standards and continual pressure to fulfill deadlines are common features of a developer's existence. Whether managing independent client work or working on a large project as part of a team, developers frequently come with scenarios with tight deadlines and high stakes. Cognitive performance may be impacted both immediately and over time by this high-stress setting.

- **Deadline Pressures:** Developers usually work on projects with tight deadlines, which force them to adjust their workflow. Mental exhaustion and ongoing stress can result from the pressure to deliver a product or solution on schedule while upholding high standards of quality. Developers may speed through code when given arbitrary timelines, which raises the possibility of errors and defects. Stress levels are further increased by the necessity to fulfill deadlines, which frequently leads to longer workdays.

- **Problem-Solving Demands:** Resolving intricate technological issues is one of the main duties of developers. These duties, which range from troubleshooting problems to creating new features, demand a lot of mental concentration and cognitive power. However, developers may become frustrated and experience cognitive overload if they are faced with an excessive amount of problems to tackle, which can impair their capacity to think creatively and make wise judgments.

- **Industry Volatility:** The technology sector is dynamic and fast-paced. It can be challenging to balance the need to learn with continuing employment obligations when developers are expected to stay current with the newest tools, languages, and technologies. The high level of stress that developers frequently experience might be exacerbated by a fear of becoming outdated or falling behind.

In these circumstances, stress sets off a series of physiological reactions that impact the body and brain. Stress can temporarily increase focus and concentration by triggering the "fight or flight" response. Chronic stress, on the other hand, has a considerably more negative effect on brain function.

6.2 The Reaction of the Brain to Prolonged Stress

Long-term exposure to stressors is known as chronic stress, and it negatively impacts several brain regions, including those involved in memory, judgment, and emotional control. Developers are particularly vulnerable to these detrimental cognitive impacts since they deal with stress on a regular basis from project demands and pressure to solve problems.

- **Impaired Memory Function:** The impact of long-term stress on memory is among its most well-established consequences. Cortisol, a hormone released in response to stress, can harm the hippocampus, the part of the brain involved in memory formation and retention, if it is present in excess. Chronic stress may make it more difficult for developers to remember important details or retain information, as their work involves recalling coding procedures, troubleshooting techniques, and project details.

- **Decreased Cognitive Flexibility:** Long-term stress also impairs cognitive flexibility, which is the capacity to adjust to new knowledge or environmental changes. Two crucial aspects of software development, creativity and problem-solving, may be difficult for developers who are under a lot of stress. A mental block brought on by this decrease in cognitive flexibility may make it difficult to come up with creative answers or to change course fast in the face of unforeseen difficulties.

- **Emotional Dysregulation:** Chronic stress also has a detrimental effect on the prefrontal cortex of the brain, which is in charge of self-control, emotional regulation, and decision-making. Long-term stress can make developers more agitated, nervous, or prone to emotional outbursts. Stress can be exacerbated by emotional dysregulation, which also affects professional performance and can damage relationships with clients and coworkers.

- **Deterioration of Mental Health:** Prolonged stress can lead to the emergence of more serious mental health conditions like burnout, depression, and anxiety disorders. A developer's capacity to perform at their best on both a professional and personal level can be significantly impacted by mental health issues in a field that requires mental clarity and sustained focus.

Chronic stress has long-term effects on quality of life and general well-being that go beyond the workplace. To safeguard their mental health and brain function, developers need to be aware of the warning signals of chronic stress and take proactive measures to lessen its impact.

6.3 Developer Stress-Reduction Strategies

Developers must integrate efficient stress-reduction strategies into their daily routines because persistent stress can have a detrimental impact on their cognitive and emotional well-being. In addition to being essential for preserving mental health, stress management also improves creativity, problem-solving skills, and cognitive function. The following are some scientifically proven techniques that developers can use to successfully handle stress:

- **Mindfulness Meditation**: One of the best methods for lowering stress and fostering mental clarity is mindfulness meditation. Developers may teach their minds to cope with stress better by concentrating on the here and now and accepting it without passing judgment. Research indicates that practicing mindfulness meditation can lower cortisol levels, increase emotional regulation, and improve attention. Even ten to fifteen minutes a day of mindfulness meditation can help developers feel less stressed and think more clearly.

- **Deep Breathing Exercises:** Stress frequently causes fast, shallow breathing, which intensifies tension and anxiety. Deep breathing techniques that can stimulate the body's parasympathetic nervous system and promote relaxation include the 4-7-8 technique and diaphragmatic breathing. These exercises can help developers relax and concentrate their attention during stressful situations, like before significant deadlines or during especially difficult coding sessions.

- Engaging in regular physical activity can significantly reduce stress and improve cognitive function. By producing endorphins, which are naturally occurring mood enhancers, frequent physical activity whether it be yoga, running, or walking helps lower stress. Exercise is a crucial component of stress management for developers since it enhances cognitive function and improves the quality of sleep. During lengthy coding sessions, even little pauses for exercise can greatly enhance mental clarity and lower stress levels.

- **Time Management and Task Prioritization**: Feeling overburdened by the amount of work is one of the primary causes of stress in developers. The secret to lowering this stress is to prioritize your tasks and manage your time well. Large projects should be divided into smaller, more manageable tasks by developers, who should also give each work a reasonable timeframe. Developers can stay organized and lessen the stress that comes with balancing several obligations by using tools like task management software (such as Trello or Asana).

- **Social Support and Communication:** Communication and social engagement are essential for stress reduction. Developers can reduce feelings of loneliness by discussing work-related difficulties with friends, mentors, and coworkers on a regular basis. Creating a support system at work or in online forums might help developers deal with stressful situations more skillfully by offering insightful counsel and emotional support.

- **Set Boundaries:** Many developers find it difficult to draw a line between their personal and professional lives in today's tech-driven world, particularly in remote work settings. Burnout might result from constant connectivity because developers may feel under pressure to answer emails or fix issues outside typical business hours. Reducing stress and avoiding burnout requires establishing clear boundaries and designating particular times for work and personal interests.

- **Adequate Sleep:** Getting enough sleep is crucial for

stress management and recovery. To enable the brain to recuperate from everyday challenges, developers should make obtaining seven to nine hours of sleep every night a priority. Establishing a sleep-friendly habit is essential for preserving emotional equilibrium and mental clarity because chronic sleep deprivation merely increases stress and affects cognitive function.

Developers can lessen the negative impacts of ongoing stress on their brain health and enhance their general well-being by putting these stress-reduction strategies into practice. Developing long-term resilience and safeguarding cognitive function throughout one's career are the goals of stress management, not only short-term mental clarity.

Although stress is an unavoidable aspect of a developer's work, prolonged stress can negatively impact performance, emotional well-being, and brain function. Development professionals can safeguard their cognitive capacities, improve their problem-solving talents, and lead more balanced, satisfying careers by being aware of how stress impacts the brain and adopting proactive measures to control it. Any developer's toolset should include stress-reduction techniques like mindfulness, exercise, social support, and time management since they support long-term brain health and maintain productivity in the demanding field of software development.

CHAPTER 7

DIET AND MENTAL WELL-BEING

Despite being crucial to general brain health and cognitive performance, nutrition is frequently disregarded, particularly by developers who work in hectic and demanding workplaces. Because of the close relationship between the mind and body, the foods developers eat during extended periods of coding can either improve or impair their mental health. This chapter examines the typical unhealthy eating patterns of development, offers dietary recommendations for items that improve brain function, and talks about the importance of being hydrated for cognitive function.

7.1 Developers' Unhealthy Eating Patterns

In the computer sector, where lengthy workdays and strict deadlines are typical, developers frequently forgo eating healthily in favor of convenience. Fast food, snacks, and sugary drinks become the go-to fuel in this workplace because of the nature of the work, which involves sitting for extended amounts of time while working on intricate coding chores. These dietary decisions, however, may have serious long-term effects on brain function.

- **Fast Food and Processed Meals:** Fast food contains a lot of sugar, processed carbs, and unhealthy fats, which can cause energy dumps and affect cognitive performance. These foods are deficient in vital nutrients that are important for brain function, including vitamins, minerals, and healthy fats. Fast food may give you a temporary energy boost, but as your blood sugar levels rise and fall, it can also cause mental sluggishness, anger, and trouble focusing.

- **Snacking on Empty Calories:** A lot of developers eat processed snacks that are heavy in sugar and salt, such as candy bars and chips, throughout the day. These "empty calories" have minimal nutritious value and can make weariness, tension, and anxiety worse. A brief increase in mental alertness may result from snacking on sugary foods, but this is followed by a dramatic drop in energy and cognitive clarity, making it more difficult to maintain concentration for extended periods of time.

- **Caffeine Overload:** Energy drinks and coffee are commonplace among developers, who use them to stay energized during late-night coding sessions or to meet project deadlines. Caffeine can improve alertness and concentration in moderation, but too much of it can have detrimental side effects like jitteriness, anxiety, and irregular sleep patterns. Heavy caffeine users may have brief spikes in productivity followed by mental meltdowns, which can affect long-term cognitive performance and cause burnout in developers.

These unhealthy eating patterns lead to the long-term deterioration of brain health in addition to having an immediate impact on mental performance. Consuming a diet low in nutrients and heavy in processed foods on a regular basis can raise the risk of memory problems, cognitive decline, and even illnesses like anxiety and depression. Developers need to understand how crucial a healthy diet is to preserving long-term cognitive function and general wellbeing.

7.2 Foods That Improve the Brain

A balanced diet full of brain-boosting nutrients can improve memory, emotional stability, and cognitive performance, just as bad nutrition can have a detrimental impact on brain health. Incorporating nutrient-dense foods into daily routines can be quite beneficial for developers, who frequently rely heavily on their mental faculties to tackle complicated challenges and stay innovative. The following are some essential meals and nutrients that have been demonstrated to promote brain health:

Omega-3 Fatty Acids: These vital fatty acids are important for preserving the structure and functionality of the brain. They are especially crucial for cognitive function and memory. Omega-3 fatty acids prevent age-related cognitive decline, lower inflammation, and aid in the growth and repair of brain cells.

- Omega-3s are abundant in fatty fish, including

sardines, mackerel, and salmon. Walnuts, chia seeds, and flaxseeds are great plant-based alternatives for people who desire them.

Antioxidants: These substances shield the brain from oxidative stress, which can harm brain tissue and hasten the deterioration of cognitive function. Antioxidants assist maintain mental clarity and shield the brain from age-related illnesses like Alzheimer's by scavenging free radicals.

- **Sources:** Antioxidants, especially flavonoids, which have been demonstrated to improve memory, are abundant in berries, including blueberries, strawberries, and raspberries. Dark chocolate (with a high cacao content) and dark leafy greens (kale, spinach) are other sources.

B Vitamins: The health and cognitive function of the brain depend on B vitamins, especially B6, B12, and folate. They aid in neurotransmitter regulation, brain fog reduction, and cellular energy production. Memory loss, disorientation, and even depression are linked to B vitamin deficiencies.

- **Sources:** B vitamins are abundant in eggs, lean

meats (such as turkey and chicken), whole grains, legumes, and dark green vegetables. Certain cereals are also enriched with these vital elements.

Vitamin E: A potent antioxidant, vitamin E aids in shielding the brain from oxidative stress. A diet high in vitamin E has been linked to better cognitive performance and a decreased risk of neurodegenerative disorders, according to studies.

- Vitamin E is abundant in nuts and seeds, including hazelnuts, sunflower seeds, and almonds. Leafy greens and avocados also contain this vitamin.

Healthy carbs: The brain needs glucose to work continuously, and healthy carbs give it energy in a steady, long-lasting way. Unlike simple sweets, complex carbs release glucose into the bloodstream gradually, giving you sustained mental energy.

- **Sources:** Legumes, vegetables like sweet potatoes, and whole grains (including quinoa, oats, and brown rice) give the brain the energy it needs to be focused and attentive.

Foods High in Protein: Protein aids in the synthesis of neurotransmitters, which are necessary for brain cell communication. Additionally, it keeps blood sugar levels stable, avoiding energy slumps during extended workdays.

- **References:** Good sources of protein that promote brain function include lean meats, fish, eggs, and plant-based foods like lentils, beans, and tofu.

Developers may maintain cognitive function, enhance mental clarity, and safeguard their long-term brain health by including these brain-boosting items in their diet. In addition to preventing mental exhaustion during long coding sessions, proper nutrition maximizes the brain's capacity for resilience, creativity, and problem-solving.

7.3 Hydration's Function

Although nutrition issues frequently overshadow the significance of hydration, keeping adequate hydration is one of the most important factors in preserving cognitive function. Since the brain is composed of over 75% water, even mild dehydration can affect one's capacity for focus, memory, and judgment.

- **Dehydration's Effect on Cognitive Function**: Mental exhaustion, slowed processing speeds, and diminished short-term memory result from the brain having to work harder to complete daily tasks when the body is dehydrated. Developers who are somewhat dehydrated may feel like they have brain fog, have more headaches, and have trouble concentrating. Chronic dehydration can eventually impair brain function and cause cognitive impairment.

- **Signs of Dehydration:** When working long hours, developers may not always notice the symptoms of dehydration. Dizziness, headaches, dry mouth, and difficulty concentrating are typical symptoms. Ignoring these symptoms might make dehydration worse and make it harder to think clearly.

Hydration Strategies:
1. **Regular Water Intake:** Drinking water often throughout the day is the easiest and most efficient method of staying hydrated. To promote frequent

hydration, developers should try to keep a water bottle close at hand while working. Since thirst is a late sign of dehydration, waiting until it occurs is not advised.

2. **Including Hydrating Foods:** Certain foods, especially fruits and vegetables with a high water content, also help you stay hydrated. Fruits that are easy to include in meals or snacks include cucumber, watermelon, oranges, and leafy greens.

3. **Restricting Dehydrating Drinks:** Although they are common in the IT industry, beverages like coffee and energy drinks can cause dehydration because of their diuretic qualities. To prevent the negative effects of dehydration on cognition, developers should balance their coffee consumption with plenty of water.

Maintaining healthy brain function requires drinking plenty of water, especially for developers who need to be able to focus and think quickly. Drinking enough water helps you think more quickly, remember things better, and solve problems more effectively. Developers may make sure their brains are working at their best by monitoring how much water they consume throughout the day.

Because of the nature of their profession, developers have particular difficulties in preserving brain health, which frequently results in bad eating habits, a dependence on fast food, and dehydration. However, people can maintain mental clarity, improve cognitive function, and guard against long-term brain health problems by consciously choosing to include brain-boosting items in their diet and drinking enough water. Making nutrition a priority helps developers stay resilient, creative, and bright throughout their careers by optimizing the mind as well as the body.

CHAPTER 8

BRAIN FATIGUE AND DIGITAL OVERLOAD

The digital environment in which developers work in the modern software development industry necessitates continuous screen time. Because of the nature of their work, they must spend hours in front of a screen without interruption, whether they are creating code, debugging, researching new frameworks, or working virtually with team members. Prolonged use of digital gadgets can result in "digital overload," a disease that, if left untreated, wears down the brain and affects cognitive performance in general. This chapter explores the impacts of continuous screen time, how information overload affects cognitive function, and useful methods for reducing digital weariness.

8.1 Continuous Screen Time

Whether on a desktop, laptop, or mobile device, displays

are the center of a developer's workday. Constant exposure to digital interfaces damages cognitive function in addition to the eyes.

- **Visual Strain:** Extended use of screens can cause eye strain, which manifests as headaches, dry eyes, impaired vision, and trouble focusing. The terms "computer vision syndrome" and "digital eye strain" are frequently used to describe this. Eye tiredness can result from the strong attention needed to read code or scan long text passages, particularly for developers working in dimly lit environments or in front of highly reflective screens.

- **Cognitive Fatigue:** Eye strain is a physical sign of digital overload, but it's just as worrying when it comes to cognitive strain. The brain is not made to handle continuous, uninterrupted streams of information. Developers need to be extremely focused when writing, debugging, or tackling intricate logic problems. This kind of prolonged mental strain can deplete cognitive reserves, resulting in mental exhaustion, diminished capacity for problem-solving, and slowed processing speeds.

- **Sleep Disruption:** When developers work late into the night, the blue light from displays might interfere with circadian cycles. Exposure to blue light inhibits the production of melatonin, which makes it more difficult to fall asleep. Memory, concentration, and creativity—the very abilities developers depend on for optimal performance—are all negatively impacted by poor sleep, in addition to physical health.

In light of these characteristics, prolonged screen use can cause both short-term discomfort and long-term cognitive loss if left unchecked. To protect their mental and physical health, developers need to take proactive measures to mitigate the risks of digital overload.

8.2 The Effects of Information Overload

Developers must deal with the difficulty of processing large volumes of data at once in addition to extended screen time. Researching code libraries, reading documentation, handling emails, and interacting with people on different platforms can all result in an overwhelming amount of information that might disrupt cognitive function.

The brain can only process so much information at a time, therefore overloading it with too much information causes attention and concentration to decline. Developers become less cognitively efficient when they are juggling many tasks, such as navigating between coding environments, browser tabs, emails, and communication tools. Cognitive fragmentation results from this phenomenon, which is frequently called "task-switching," in which the brain finds it difficult to focus on one topic at a time before being drawn into another. Tasks take longer to finish as a result, and the caliber of the work declines.

Decision fatigue can result from continuously assessing new information, choosing how to prioritize tasks, and figuring out the best course of action. Over time, poorer decision-making results from decision fatigue, which happens when the brain is overloaded with options. This could result in developers choosing less effective code methods, making logical mistakes, or finding it difficult to come up with original solutions to problems.

Mental tiredness: In addition to impairing concentration, information overload also plays a role in mental tiredness. Developers who work in fast-paced settings frequently experience pressure to stay up to date with project deadlines, industry trends, and changing technology. There is little time for mental healing because of the constant barrage of information and the requirement to stay current with the newest frameworks and technologies. This can eventually result in burnout, which leaves developers feeling emotionally and physically exhausted and less inspired and creative.

When developers try to handle too much information at once, it leads to a vicious cycle of cognitive fatigue, poor productivity, and higher errors. To maintain long-term cognitive performance, developers must be aware of the negative consequences of multitasking and consuming too much information.

8.3 Methods for Reducing Digital Fatigue

Developers must use techniques that encourage cognitive recovery and reduce the detrimental effects of extended screen time and information overload in order to fight digital overload and brain fatigue. The following useful methods for enhancing mental and physical well-being are simple to incorporate into daily routines:

- **Screen Breaks:** Taking regular screen breaks is one of the best strategies to reduce eye strain and avoid cognitive fatigue. The 20-20-20 rule is an often suggested method:
    - stare at anything 20 feet away for 20 seconds every 20 minutes. This lowers the chance of computer vision syndrome and permits the eyes to relax. Furthermore, taking frequent, brief pauses from the screen improves focus and helps the brain recover before returning to work.

- **Digital Detoxes:** Developers can gain from purposeful digital detoxes in which they spend a lot of time away from screens, particularly after work. This can involve doing screen-free activities like working out, reading books, or going outside. On the weekends or in the evenings, taking a digital detox enhances the quality of sleep and aids in the brain's recovery from continuous stimulation.

- **Pomodoro Technique**: This time-management strategy promotes concentrated work sessions interspersed with brief breaks. Developers work in "Pomodoros" (25-minute blocks) and then take 5-minute breaks. A longer 15–30 minute break is taken after four Pomodoros. By including regular breaks, this method prevents burnout and encourages sustained focus during work sessions. Developers can sustain cognitive acuity throughout the day by striking a balance between focused and relaxed hours.

- **Optimizing the Work Environment:** Reducing the physical strain caused by screen time requires an ergonomic and aesthetically pleasing workspace. To lessen glare, developers should spend money on top-notch displays with movable brightness and contrast settings. Wearing blue light-blocking glasses or applying blue light filters can further lessen the negative effects of extended screen time, especially at night. In order to encourage good posture and lessen neck and back strain, which can exacerbate general weariness, developers should also make sure that their workstations are ergonomically constructed.

- **Mindfulness and Meditation:** Stress can be considerably decreased and cognitive resilience enhanced by including mindfulness exercises like meditation into regular routines. By lowering the propensity to multitask and clearing out mental clutter, mindfulness aids developers in remaining in the present. Focus, mood, and the mental fatigue brought on by digital overload can all be improved by setting aside a short period of time each day to engage in guided meditation or deep breathing techniques.

- **Limiting Multitasking:** By lowering the desire to

multitask, developers can increase cognitive efficiency. This can be accomplished by shutting down unused tabs in the browser, turning off notifications that aren't absolutely necessary, and setting aside certain time slots for specific tasks. One way to avoid cognitive fragmentation and preserve mental clarity is to schedule specific time for coding and different times for responding to emails or attending meetings.

- **Using Digital Wellness apps:** A number of digital wellness apps are available to track and limit screen usage. While productivity applications such as "Focus@Will" play background music intended to improve focus, apps like "Flux" change the color temperature of screens to lessen exposure to blue light. By tracking the amount of time spent on various applications and websites, other solutions such as "RescueTime" give developers insight into their digital habits and help them make changes to prevent burnout.

Developers can improve focus, lower the danger of

burnout, and stop digital overload from affecting cognitive function by implementing these tactics into their daily routines. Even while the digital world is an essential component of contemporary development work, long-term brain health depends on striking a balance.

Developers are more susceptible to digital overload and brain fatigue in today's tech-driven workplace because of the continual screen time and deluge of information. However, developers can safeguard their mental and physical well-being by being aware of the detrimental effects these factors have on cognitive function and putting useful tactics into practice, like taking screen breaks, controlling information intake, and improving work surroundings. Adopting a balanced approach to digital engagement is essential for long-term success and wellbeing because it allows the brain to relax and recuperate from the pressures of a fast-paced, screen-dominated environment.

CHAPTER 9

WORK-LIFE BALANCE'S SIGNIFICANCE

The pursuit of perfection in the fast-paced field of software development frequently causes the lines between work and personal life to blur. An unsustainable imbalance may result from developers sacrificing personal time due to deadline pressure, the need for continuous availability, and the "hustle" mentality. This chapter highlights the vital requirement for work-life balance while examining the complex effects of this imbalance on mental health and individual well-being.

9.1 The Stress of Personal Sacrifice and Deadlines

The drive to produce high-quality work and fulfill deadlines can result in major personal compromises in many development contexts. This section looks at the effects of these demands on general wellbeing and cognitive function.

- **Mental Strain:** The constant pressure to meet deadlines can lead to a high-stress workplace where developers feel pressured to put in long hours and neglect their personal obligations. Burnout, which is characterized by emotional tiredness, cynicism, and decreased productivity, can result from this mental strain. Chronic stress can worsen memory, attention, and decision-making skills, according to studies, which makes developers' jobs even more difficult.

- **Risks to Physical Health:** Extended durations of high-pressure work might cause physical health to be neglected. To fulfill project requirements, many developers may forgo meals, exercise, or sleep. Neglect like this can lead to weight gain, exhaustion, and other health problems, which can further impair cognitive function and productivity at work. Furthermore, coding's sedentary nature raises the risk of diseases like obesity, heart disease, and musculoskeletal ailments.

- **The decline of interpersonal relationships:**

Relationship tension with family and friends frequently arises from the sacrifice of personal time. Social ties may suffer when job takes precedence, which can result in feelings of loneliness and isolation. Depression and anxiety may result from this emotional detachment, which can also have an adverse effect on mental health. When personal ties deteriorate, developers may feel overwhelmed and unsupported. Personal relationships are essential for resilience and emotional support.

- **Job Satisfaction and Retention:** Lowered job satisfaction may result from constant pressure to perform at work without proper work-life balance. Developers who feel overworked and underappreciated might look for job elsewhere, which would increase an organization's turnover rate. Businesses that disregard the value of work-life balance may find it more and more difficult to keep top staff, which could lead to a loss of continuity and experience.

9.2 Leisure's Contribution to Cognitive Health

Even though work takes up a large portion of a developer's life, leisure activities are essential for supporting cognitive health and mental healing. The cognitive advantages of hobbies, sports, and leisure are highlighted in this section.

- **Mental Recovery**: Recreational pursuits offer a vital chance for mental recuperation, enabling developers to disconnect from the pressures of the workplace and replenish their mental reserves. By stimulating various parts of the brain, hobbies and leisure activities help to promote neuroplasticity, or the brain's capacity to change and rearrange itself. In order to avoid burnout and improve general cognitive function, this mental vacation is essential.

- The ability to solve problems in development work requires creativity, which can be increased by engaging in recreational activities. Divergent thinking the capacity to come up with original solutions is fostered by pastimes that require artistic expression, such as writing, painting, or performing music. In the end, both the individual and the company might gain from creative solutions to software development problems brought about by this cognitive flexibility.

- **Reduction of Stress:** Leisure activities are a natural remedy for stress. Exercise and other physical activity release endorphins, which are the body's natural stress relievers and enhance emotions of happiness and wellbeing. Furthermore, relaxing pastimes like reading, gardening, or meditation can reduce cortisol levels, lessening the physiological effects of stress. Reduced stress is linked to better brain health and cognitive performance.

- **Social Connection:** Whether it's through team sports, group classes, or common interests, leisure activities frequently offer chances for social connection. Resilience and emotional well-being depend on establishing and preserving social ties. In order to maintain cognitive function and general well-being, positive social connections can improve mood, lessen feelings of loneliness, and offer support during trying times.

9.3 Setting Work and Life Boundaries

To support brain health and improve general life pleasure, it is essential to draw distinct lines between work and leisure time. The methods for successfully establishing these borders are examined in this section.

The implementation of efficient time management strategies can help developers distinguish between work and personal time. Maintaining a healthy work-life balance can be facilitated by creating a regular daily schedule that includes assigned work hours, breaks, and leisure time. Setting priorities for work and making sure that personal commitments are kept can be facilitated by using tools like calendars, task organizers, and time-tracking applications.

- **Designated Workspaces:** Establishing a specific area for work, whether at home or in the workplace, can help to strengthen the lines between personal and professional life. A clear workplace tells the brain when it's time to concentrate on work-related activities, and leaving it marks the start of personal time. While encouraging leisure and relaxation outside of work hours, this physical separation can assist minimize distractions and increase productivity during working hours.

- **Establishing Boundaries for Communication:** Developers should establish limits on communication, especially after work hours, in order to preserve work-life balance. A psychological separation from work can be achieved by establishing "offline" times when emails, messages, and other work-related correspondence are not checked. Sharing these limits with coworkers and superiors promotes a respectful work environment and inspires others to follow suit.

- **Prioritizing Self-Care:** Maintaining general well-being requires prioritizing self-care. Developers ought to set aside time for pursuits like exercise, hobbies, relaxation methods, and interacting with friends and family that support both mental and physical well-being. Frequent self-care routines can boost mood, increase energy levels, and improve cognitive function, all of which contribute to increased output and job satisfaction.

- **Encouraging a Supportive Work Culture:** By cultivating a supportive work culture, organizations can significantly contribute to the advancement of work-life balance. Developer stress can be lessened by fostering health programs, providing flexible work schedules, and encouraging candid conversations regarding workload. Businesses that prioritize work-life balance are more likely to boost employee morale, retain talent, and increase overall productivity.

It is beneficial for developers to schedule frequent check-ins with themselves in order to evaluate their work-life balance. Examining one's workload, stress levels, and personal obligations might help identify areas that could need modification. In order to maintain a better balance, these check-ins help developers become more self-aware and motivate them to make the required adjustments.

The pressure to produce high-quality work and meet deadlines in the software development industry frequently results in the loss of personal time, which has a negative impact on one's general well-being and brain health. Maintaining cognitive function, improving job satisfaction, and preserving interpersonal connections all depend on an understanding of the significance of work-life balance. In order to create an atmosphere that supports both professional achievement and personal fulfillment, developers should prioritize leisure activities, set clear limits, and cultivate a friendly work culture. In order to achieve a healthier, happier, and more productive existence, the pursuit of work-life balance is a continuous process that calls for dedication, self-awareness, and a readiness to accept change.

CHAPTER 10

DEVELOPING HEALTHFUL ROUTINES FOR LONG-TERM MENTAL WELL-BEING

It is more important than ever for engineers to put their mental health first as the software development industry changes. Adopting healthy habits is crucial for preserving cognitive function and general well-being in a field that is marked by high mental demands and quick technological developments. This chapter offers a thorough manual for creating a healthy routine, integrating mental and social stimulation, and comprehending the long-term advantages of leading a balanced lifestyle.

10.1 Establishing a Healthful Habit

The cornerstone of cognitive health is a regimented schedule that prioritizes good behaviors. With a focus on three important areas: sleep, exercise, and a healthy diet this section offers developers helpful guidance on how to establish and sustain routines that support brain health.

Prioritizing sleep is essential for brain health since it affects cognitive function, emotional control, and memory consolidation. Developers should try to get between seven and nine hours of sleep per night and think about doing the following:

1. The body's internal clock can be regulated by sleeping at the same time every day and waking up at the same time. Consistency improves the quality of sleep by supporting the body's normal sleep-wake cycle.
2. **Building a Sleep-Conducive Environment:** A quiet, cold, and dark room can greatly enhance the quality of your sleep. To reduce disruptions, developers might think about using sleep masks, white noise generators, or blackout curtains.
3. **Restricting Screen Time Before Bed:** The hormone that controls sleep, melatonin, may be disrupted by the blue light that screens emit. Better sleep can be achieved by limiting screen usage at least one hour before bed.

Including Frequent Exercise: Exercise is important for cognitive function in addition to promoting physical health. Exercise promotes neuroplasticity, improves blood flow to the brain, and triggers the production of neurotrophic factors. At least 150 minutes a week of moderate-intensity aerobic exercise should be the goal for developers. This should include:

1. **Aerobic Exercises:** Exercise that releases endorphins, such as swimming, cycling, or brisk walking, improves cardiovascular health and elevates happiness.
2. **Strength Training:** By increasing muscular mass and strength, resistance training can mitigate the harmful consequences of extended periods of inactivity, which are prevalent in the IT sector.
3. **Incorporating Movement into Daily Life:** Small adjustments like standing when working, walking meetings, or using the stairs can have a big impact on physical activity levels.

A diet that is well-balanced is essential for maintaining cognitive health. Foods high in nutrients give the brain the vital vitamins and minerals it needs to perform at its best. Developers ought to think about:

1. **Putting Whole Foods First:** Promoting lean proteins, whole grains, fruits, vegetables, and healthy fats helps maintain brain function. Particularly advantageous foods include those high in vitamins (such B vitamins, vitamin E, and vitamin D), omega-3 fatty acids, and antioxidants.
2. **Meal Planning and Prep:** Developers can steer clear of poor food choices during hectic work days by planning meals in advance. Maintaining healthy eating habits is made easier by preparing nutritious snacks such chopped veggies, yogurt, or nuts.
3. Maintaining proper hydration is crucial for cognitive performance. It is important for developers to stay hydrated throughout the day because even slight dehydration can affect cognitive function and focus.

10.2 Including Mental and Social Input

Social relationships, mental difficulties, and physical wellness all contribute to improved cognitive health. In order to support sustained cognitive function, this section addresses strategies for promoting lifelong learning and social ties.

Building Social Connections: Better emotional and cognitive health are associated with strong social ties. Developers ought to make an effort to build connections both within and outside of the office:

1. Building professional relationships and networking with others in the field encourages cooperation, idea exchange, and emotional support. Developers can make valuable relationships by going to conferences, workshops, or meetups.
2. **Personal Relationships:** Socializing with loved ones can ease stress and offer emotional support. Developers ought to place a high value on spending time with their loved ones and doing things that deepen their relationships.
3. Engaging in group activities, such as joining clubs, sports teams, or community groups, promotes mental health by fostering social connection and offering chances for shared experiences.

Encouraging Lifelong Learning: Ongoing education

promotes neuroplasticity and improves cognitive performance by stimulating the brain. Developers ought to seize the chance to learn both inside and outside of their fields of expertise:

1. **Pursuing Professional Development:** You can improve your knowledge and abilities by enrolling in classes, going to workshops, or being certified. In addition to helping with job advancement, keeping up with industry trends keeps the mind sharp and interested.

2. **Exploring New Hobbies:** Trying new things, like painting, playing an instrument, or taking up a sport, can encourage creativity and stimulate various brain processes. The brain remains active and flexible due to the novelty of new experiences.

3. **Reading and Intellectual Engagement**: Reading books, articles, or journals that are pertinent to one's professional or personal interests can encourage critical thinking and cognitive engagement. Having conversations about what has been read improves understanding and memory as well.

10.3 The Advantages of a Balanced Lifestyle Over Time

Developing healthy habits has several long-term advantages for cognitive function, brain health, and general professional achievement. These advantages are outlined in this section, which also highlights the significance of leading a balanced lifestyle.

- **Improved Cognitive Ability:** Maintaining a healthy lifestyle enhances memory, focus, and problem-solving skills by promoting optimal brain function. Neurogenesis, or the creation of new neurons, is facilitated by regular exercise, a healthy diet, and enough sleep, all of which improve cognitive resilience.

- **Improved Emotional Well-Being:** A balanced lifestyle is associated with improved mental health, which lessens depressive and anxious symptoms. A happy attitude on life is fostered by social relationships and participation in rewarding activities, which support emotional stability and resilience.

- **Increased Productivity and Performance:** Professional productivity is positively correlated with healthy behaviors. Developers who put their health first are more creative, motivated, and focused, which produces better work and leads to more professional success.

- **Resilience Against Cognitive loss:** Maintaining a healthy lifestyle can help reduce the chance of aging-related cognitive loss. Regular exercise, preserving social ties, and pushing the brain through education all contribute to the development of a cognitive reserve, which acts as a preventative measure against age-related decline.

- **Sustainable Career Satisfaction:** Developers who put their health and wellbeing first are probably going to have longer career longevity and higher job satisfaction. A satisfying working experience that is consistent with personal beliefs is produced when a favorable work-life balance is combined with efficient stress management and self-care techniques.

Developers who want to maintain long-term brain health and cognitive performance must adopt healthy behaviors. Developers can improve their cognitive function and general well-being by establishing a healthy routine that places an emphasis on sleep, exercise, and a balanced diet, cultivating social relationships, and embracing lifelong learning. The pursuit of a balanced lifestyle is a continuous endeavor with significant rewards, culminating in a rewarding and prosperous profession in the dynamic field of software development. In the end, taking care of one's health is not only an investment in one's own wellbeing; it is also a critical tactic for attaining resilience and professional competence in a demanding field.

ABOUT THE AUTHOR

Technology specialist and author Emma Royce Smartley specializes in the newest developments in AI, coding tools, and software development. His goal as a writer is to help developers and tech fans remain ahead of the curve by simplifying difficult tech ideas. His publications provide insightful analyses of how new technologies are changing the landscape of productivity and software development. Emma's love of innovation propels him to investigate and elucidate the technologies that will shape the landscape of the future.

www.ingramcontent.com/pod-product-compliance
Lightning Source LLC
Chambersburg PA
CBHW050323230526
45471CB00005B/2329